WORLD RELIGIONS

JUDAISM

Angela Wood

Thomson Learning
New York

Words appearing in *italic* in the text have not fallen into common English usage. The publishers have followed Merriam Webster's Collegiate Dictionary (Tenth Edition) for spelling and usage.

First published in the United States in 1995 by
Thomson Learning
New York, NY

Published simultaneously in Great Britain by Wayland (Publishers) Ltd.

U.S. copyright © 1995 Thomson Learning

U.K. copyright © 1995 Wayland Publishers Ltd.

Library of Congress Cataloging-in-Publication Data
Wood, Angela.
  Judaism / Angela Wood.
      p.   cm.—(World religions)
  Summary: An illustrated history and explanation of the beliefs and practices of Judaism.
  Includes bibliographical references and index.
  ISBN 1-56847-376-1
  1. Judaism—Juvenile literature. [1. Judaism.] I. Title.
  II. Series.
  BM573.W66   1995
  296—dc20   95–1943

Printed in Italy

Acknowledgments

The author thanks the following for contributing to the book, by talking about their lives as Jews, having their photographs taken, making helpful suggestions, and, above all, by their encouragement and excitement: Jeremy Angel, the Berak family, the Bower Ish-Horowicz family, Libby Burkeman, Yosef Chernobilsky, John Curtis, Samuel Gilmore, Ester Gluck, Marcus Graichen, David Gryn, Rabbi Hugo Gryn, Mehri Niknam, Lenny Nead, the Oppenheimer family, Philip Ratner, Solomon Sananes, the Silverman family, Maxwell Simon, Rabbi Jacqueline Tabick, Desi Tammam, the children of Welwyn Garden City Synagogue, U.K.

The author and publishers thank the following for their permission to reproduce photographs: Gordon Charatan: p. 34; Circa Photo Library: p. 41 (bottom); Anne Frank Stiftung: p. 12; Guy Hall: *title page, contents page,* 6 (bottom), 28, 32, 41 (top), 45 (top); Robert Harding Picture Library: pp. 7 (ASAP/Aliza Auerbach), 23 (ASAP/Joel Fishman), 33 (PHOTRI), 35 (ASAP/J. Kaszemacher), 38 (ASAP/Israel Talby), 44 (PHOTRI); Hutchison Library (Liba Taylor): pp. 6 (top), 30; Christine Osborne: pp. 5, 10, 13, 22, 24, 36 (bottom); TRIP: pp. 19 (M. O'Brien-Thumm), 21 (A. and B. Peerless), 29 (R. Cracknell), 36 (top) (H. Rogers), 37 (H. Rogers); Welwyn Garden City Hebrew Congregation: p. 45 (bottom); Women's International Zionist Organization: pp. 15, 18. The photos on pp. 4, 8, 9, 15 (top), 20, 25, 26, 31, 39, and 40 were taken by Angela Wood.

Cover photo: Lighting the Shabbat candles.
Title page: A Jewish mother draws in the light of the Shabbat candles.
Contents page: A rabbi shows two young people the Torah scroll. "Turn it and turn it for everything is in it."

Contents

THE HEBREW LANGUAGE

Around the world, Jews use Hebrew for prayers and Jewish study. In Israel, Hebrew is also the main everyday language of Jewish people. Jewish children there also learn Arabic and English in school.

INTRODUCTION

Who is a Jew?

There is a simple answer to this question. A Jew is someone who has a Jewish mother or who chooses to become Jewish. There are also more complicated answers.

Being Jewish is religious: believing in one God, praying to God, keeping "Shabbat" (the Sabbath) as a special day…

Being Jewish is cultural: enjoying Jewish songs, eating special foods, using certain expressions…

Being Jewish is historical: belonging to a people that is four thousand years old and understanding that events in the past affect life today…

Being Jewish is social: being with other Jews and doing things together that help Jews be Jewish…

Being Jewish is political: being part of a people all over the world, with a spiritual homeland in Israel, and feeling that whatever happens to any Jew somehow happens to all Jews.

Absorbed in prayer at the Western Wall in the Old City of Jerusalem. This is the nearest spot to the site of the First Temple. Many Jews go to pray there, in groups or alone.

Observance

Many Jews are "observant": that is, they lead a religious life. They practice their religion and culture in different ways, and there are various groups to which they might belong. For example, some Jews are members of Orthodox synagogues but are not fully observant in their private lives, and some are members of Progressive synagogues but may be as observant in their private lives. Members of one family may belong to different groups, and some Jews relate to one group in one way and another group in another way.

These Hasidic Jews are choosing myrtle for the festival of Sukkot. The man on the right has a soft bag in which he carries his "tallit" (prayer shawl).

Orthodox Jews believe that the Torah (teaching) was given by God and can never change. They follow all the laws of their religion exactly. They pray in Hebrew, the language in which the Torah was written. Men and women have distinct and definite roles and responsibilities.

Reform Jews believe that the Torah has to be viewed in a new way in every age. Some Jewish laws were made by people, not by God, so the those laws can be changed. Reform Jews today keep more traditions than they used to. In Europe, there are also Liberal Jews, whose ideas are very similar to Reform. Sometimes Reform and Liberal Jews are called Progressive.

ZIONISTS

Many Jews are Zionists. They support the State of Israel and its right to exist. They see Israel as a place of refuge and also as a place of inspiration. They give money for immigrants in Israel or for environmental projects, such as tree planting. Some Zionists live in Israel.

Non-Zionists sometimes hold the Zionists responsible for the actions of the Israeli government.

5

The shofar (ram's horn) is blown on Rosh Hashanah (the New Year).

Conservative Jews accept the idea that the Torah is given by God, but they also believe that the religion must change if it is to be fully alive. They say that Jewish life can draw from other cultures and yet remain distinctly Jewish. Conservative Jews live mostly in the United States; in other countries, such as Israel and Great Britain, they are called Masorti (traditional).

There are also Jews who are pleased to be Jewish and join in many celebrations, but who do not practice their religion completely. Some do not practice at all. Some do not believe in God. Some believe in God but find the Jewish religion too difficult to observe or think that it has not adapted enough to the modern world. They are called "secular" or "cultural" Jews.

The Jewish people

In Ancient Hebrew, there was no word for *Judaism* or even for *religion*. The Hebrew word for the Jewish way of life, following Jewish law, is *halaha*, which means "way."

Sometimes people talk about the "Jewish race," but there is really no such thing. Nor is there a "Jewish nation." It is more accurate to speak about the "Jewish people." There are Jews of every race and nationality.

For the festival of Purim, many Jews wear costumes. When the story of Esther is read, they wave rattles or boo and hiss whenever Haman's name is said.

1
JEWISH HISTORY

The Jewish people have a long history, and their religion and culture have changed gradually over thousands of years. There have been several turning points. Each turning point reveals something about how Jews see the world and their place in it.

"Abraham our father"

Abraham lived in the Middle East about four thousand years ago. People then believed in different gods for different parts of life. They made idols and prayed to them. Abraham saw life as a whole, with everyone and everything connected. He believed there was only one God.

According to the Bible, Abraham heard God telling him to take his family to a new place and start a new life, with new ideas. He took them to Canaan, where they became the Hebrews. The language they spoke, Hebrew, is still the main Jewish religious language. The word means "crossing over," for it is said every Jew "crosses over" to be with God. When a person is initiated into Judaism, she or he takes a Hebrew name, such as Rachel or Noah, and is called "(Hebrew name), daughter/son of Abraham our father."

The children of Israel

Abraham and Sarah had twin grandsons, Esau and Jacob. Jacob was jealous of Esau, who would inherit the authority of the family because he was minutes older than Jacob. Jacob deceived their father and tricked Esau out of his birthright, then ran away, scared.

An Arab and a Jew greet each other in Jerusalem.

JEWS AND MUSLIMS

Abraham had a son, Isaac, by his Hebrew wife, Sarah, and a son, Ishmael, by his Egyptian wife, Hagar. The Jews descended from Isaac and the Muslims from Ishmael. Many Jews today who care about peace between Arabs and Israelis—and between Muslims and Jews—consider Arabs and Muslims to be their spiritual cousins.

7

Years later, he gained the courage to face Esau again. The night before they met, Jacob wrestled with a mysterious being in his sleep. He heard God say that he would be known from then on as "Israel," meaning someone who had struggled with God and survived. Jacob's descendants are called "the children of Israel," and many Jews feel that it is a good name for them. Sometimes they struggle with God, questioning and wondering. Sometimes they struggle for God, trying to live by the rules of the Torah.

Israel is also the name of the land where the Jews settled. Today it is the only Jewish state in the world and is a homeland for many Jews.

Ben Yehuda Street in the New City of Jerusalem. Lubavitch Jews campaign to get Jews to observe their religion more fully. Lubavitchers are the only group of Jews to campaign in this way. Here a young Jew has been persuaded to put on tefillin (small leather boxes containing Torah passages) and say his morning prayers. Ben Yehuda Street is named after Eliezer ben Yehuda, the "father of modern Hebrew." He founded the Hebrew Language Council in 1888.

"Moses our teacher"

About 3,200 years ago, the children of Israel were slaves in Egypt. Then a series of miraculous events took place, and they were freed. Moses led them toward the promised land, Israel. Accoring to scripture, on the way God gave Moses the "Torah," the teaching by which the Jewish people live.

Jerusalem: exile and return

In about 1000 C.E. the people made Jerusalem on Mount Zion their capital and built a beautiful temple where priests offered sacrifices to God. Four hundred years later, the Babylonians conquered them, destroyed the temple, and took some people away. In Babylon, the people missed their temple and worshiped locally. They wrote a song about their sadness:

"By the streams of Babylon, there we sat and wept as we thought of Zion…How shall we sing the Lord's song in a strange land? If I forget you, O Jerusalem, let my right hand wither! Let my tongue stick to my palate if I cease to remember you, if I do not set Jerusalem above my highest joy." *(Psalm 137: 1–5)*

Prophets are people who communicate with God in a special way. The prophet Jeremiah sent a letter, in the name of God, from Jerusalem to the exiles in Babylon. He told them to go on with their lives and never to lose hope. They took his advice. After 70 years, they were allowed to return to Jerusalem, but most of them stayed in Babylon. Since then, there have always been more Jews living outside Israel than inside.

A new temple was built in Jerusalem and, for a few hundred years, there were two main kinds of worship: sacrifices in the temple; and meetings, study, and prayer in synagogues. Then, about two thousand years ago, the Romans occupied Israel and destroyed the temple.

JEREMIAH'S ADVICE

"Build houses and live in them, plant gardens and eat their produce… Multiply there and do not decrease. Seek the welfare of the city to which I have exiled you and pray to God on its behalf, for in its prosperity you shall prosper."
(Jeremiah 29: 5–7)

In the New City of Jerusalem there is a model of the ancient walled city, as it was before the Second Temple was destroyed in 70 C.E.

JEWISH HISTORY

B.C.E.

2000   Abraham and his people journey from Ur to Canaan.

1200   Escape from slavery in Egypt; giving of the Torah; entry into Israel.

1000   King David makes Jerusalem the capital of Israel.

900   King Solomon builds the First Temple in Jerusalem. The Jewish community in Ethiopia may date from this time.

586   Babylonians destroy the temple and deport Jews.

? 200   Jews settle in India.

168   Syrian Greeks occupy Israel, take over the temple for idol worship, and try to make Jews abandon their religion. The Maccabees, Jewish freedom fighters, defeat them.

The festival of Hanukkah recalls the restoration of temple worship in 168 B.C.E. Candles are lit to recall the miracle of the oil, which, though only a small amount, lasted eight days.

Torah and Talmud

After the arrival of the Romans, Jews were dispersed through the Middle East and Europe. They created synagogues wherever they settled.

Study of the Torah became increasingly important, and wise or learned men who could teach about it were called "rabbis" (teachers). Most rabbis also had everyday jobs, in order to earn a living. By the first century C.E., other people met to discuss the Torah. Their discussions were remembered and written down, and later generations studied these written accounts. The collection of discussions and decisions is called the Talmud.

10

C.E.

70   Romans destroy the Second Temple and Jews are dispersed.

200   Yehudah HaNasi compiles and edits the first part of the Talmud, the Mishnah. The Talmud text is completed in the year 500.

711   Muslims rule Spain, and Jewish life flourishes freely.

1040 - In France, Rabbi Shlomo ben Yitzhak (Rashi) explains the Torah and
1105   Talmud in clear language. His commentaries are the most important in the Jewish world.

1135 - In Spain, Rabbi Moses ben Maimon (The Rambam or Maimonides)
1204   creates many works to explain Jewish laws and beliefs. These codes are still used today.

1215   The Pope orders Jews in Europe to wear a yellow badge and an ugly hat so that Christians can recognize and avoid them. Over the next centuries, Jews are forced to live in closed areas, which become known as ghettos.

"THE GOLDEN AGE OF SPAIN"

There were Jews in Spain from the first century C.E. Spain became Christian during the Roman Empire, and Jews were treated well at first, but they were severely persecuted under Christian rule from 612. In 711, Muslim Arabs conquered Spain and, although they did not see Jews as their equals, they treated them more fairly and respected them for their abilities. Jews spoke Arabic, and some had important jobs in Spanish society—for example, as doctors or translators. Jews had good relations with Muslims and could worship freely. This period is known as "The Golden Age of Spain." Soon after, Spain became Christian again. In the twelfth century, Church leaders tried to convert Jews to Christianity. Many Jews were killed because they refused. Others kept their religion secretly and pretended to be Christian to save their lives. In 1492 the Jews were driven out of Spain.

Note:
B.C.E. means Before the Common Era. C.E. means in the Common Era. (See further explanation on page 47.)

JEWISH HISTORY

1492 The Christian King and Queen of Spain expel Jews and Muslims.

1654 Jews settle in North America.

1700 – The Baal Shem Tov (Master of the Good Name) becomes the founder
1760 of the Hasidic movement in Poland. Hasidic Jews stress the joy of living a Jewish life, expressing this in song, story, and dance. Reverence for the rabbi is very important.

1806 Napoleon encourages a Jewish assembly to be created in France, showing that Jews are equal to others: the beginning of the modern period, the Enlightenment.

1835 Abraham Geiger, a German rabbi, recommends many changes in Jewish practice. Reform Judaism dates from this time.

1881 Pogroms, organized attacks on Jews, take place in Russia and neighboring countries. Many Jews are killed or expelled; many emigrate, mainly to the United States.

The Shoah

The Holocaust (1933–45) is perhaps the most tragic of all the persecutions of Jews. Its Hebrew name, Shoah, means "whirlwind." The Nazis did not want Jews to become Christian or to change in any way. They wanted them dead and had a plan to make the world free of Jews. They built concentration camps and killed six million Jews. This was almost all the Jews in Europe and about one-third of the world Jewish population at the time. Nazis also killed six million other people that they thought were "subhuman," including gypsies, the physically disabled, and the mentally ill.

Anne Frank's family hid from the Nazis in Holland, where Anne kept a diary. Only her father survived the concentration camps.

1897 In Switzerland, Theodor Herzl convenes the First Zionist Congress, an international meeting of Jews to discuss ideas for a modern Jewish homeland in Israel.

1917 The British government issues the Balfour Declaration, promising the Jews a national homeland in Palestine.

1933 Nazis come to power in Germany; Holocaust begins.

1948 The State of Israel is created and declared as a homeland for all Jews. Refugees arrive. Surrounding countries declare war on Israel and capture the Old City of Jerusalem.

1967 The Six Day War: surrounding countries attack Israel. Israel captures the West Bank from Jordan and the Gaza Strip from Egypt. The Old and New Cities of Jerusalem are reunited.

1982 Israel signs a peace agreement with Egypt. The Peace Process begins.

1994 Israel signs peace agreements with the Palestinians and with Jordan. Palestinians begin limited self-rule in part of the West Bank and the Gaza Strip.

In concentration camps and on forced marches, Jews sang a Yiddish song, *"Zog Nit Keynmol"* ("Never Say You Walk the Final Way"). It is often sung at services to remember those who died in the Shoah. Its first verse is:

We must never lose our courage
in the fight
though skies of lead turn days of
sunshine into night,
because the hour for which we've
yearn'd will yet arrive
and our marching steps will thunder:
we survive!

The Silent Scream, *a sculpture in the gardens of Yad V'Shem, a museum of the Shoah, in Israel. A Jewish visitor has left a stone in the folds of the figure's clothes, as is the custom when visiting a grave.*

The past and the future

From every age, something lives on and can be seen and felt in Jewish life today. For Jews, the most important part of history is not the past but the future. They look forward rather than look back. They hope for a time of peace, justice, and freedom for everyone, which they call "the days of the Messiah." This verse is used in Jewish prayers and sums up this belief:

"I believe with perfect faith in the coming of the Messiah and, even should it take a long time, I still believe."

HER FATHER'S DAUGHTER

This true story shows how Jewish people feel about their history and identity. Alice was nine when she heard about Jews at school. She could not figure out who they were, so her father told her about the Jewish people, from far back to the present day. She was fascinated by the fortunes of the Jewish people. "Are there any Jews alive now?" she asked. Her father replied that there were millions. Alice longed to meet Jews and discover how they survived. "Do you know any Jews?" she asked. "Yes...and so do you!" "Who? Who?" Desperate to know, she was angry with her father for only answering, "One day you'll know..." A few months later, quite suddenly, Alice's father died. Years later, she discovered that he was Jewish, although her mother was not. His family had suffered greatly because they were Jews, and many of them had been killed. Her mother had not wanted him or the family to suffer any more and had asked him to keep it a secret; he loved her very much and had agreed. Alice found out all she could about Jews. As a young woman, she was bat mitzvahed, "to remember what my father might have forgotten."

2

THE WORLD
OF JEWRY

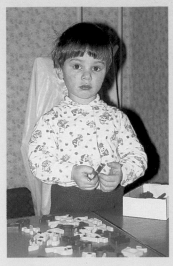

The Jewish people originated in the land of Israel, but now live all over the world. Jews do not try to convert people to their religion. They have spread mainly because they have been expelled from many countries or because they have chosen to leave places where it was hard to live a Jewish life.

In the nineteenth and twentieth centuries, many Jews emigrated to Israel. This returning to Israel is called aliyah (going up). Some go to escape persecution; some wanted to return to the place where they feel that their people are meant to be; and some feel it is more natural for Jews to be together where they can be Jewish in everything they do. Some Jews could make aliyah but do not, because they think that they can support Israel better by living outside or that being Jewish means having good relationships with other peoples—which would not happen as easily if every Jew lived in Israel.

Yosef Chernobilsky was born in 1984 in the former Soviet Union. His parents were refuseniks, Jews who were refused permission to leave the country. His father was imprisoned many times for protesting against the Soviet authorities' cruel treatment of Jews and for asking to live in Israel. His mother taught Hebrew secretly; she was never caught. Quite suddenly, in 1990, the family was allowed to leave. They now live in Israel. In the photograph, Yosef, age 4, is playing with plastic Hebrew letters, a present from relatives in the West.

Left: A refugee arriving in Israel from the war-torn city of Sarajevo is reunited with a friend, who had settled there two months before.

JEWISH POPULATIONS AROUND THE WORLD

In 1991 there were an estimated 13,973,445 Jews in the world. The largest groups were in the United States, Israel, and the former USSR.

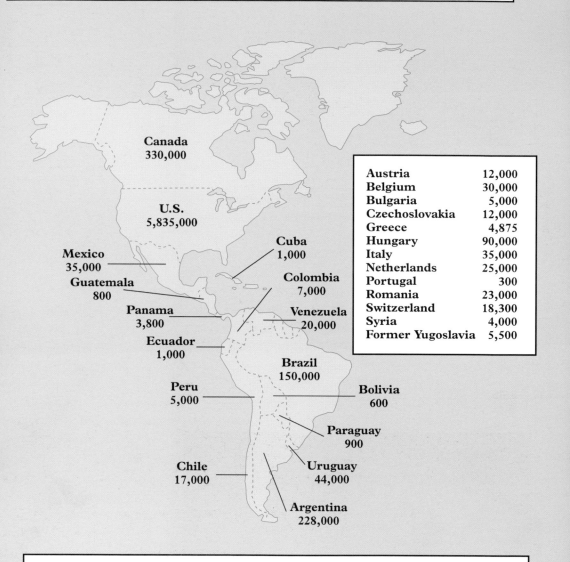

Canada
330,000

U.S.
5,835,000

Mexico
35,000

Guatemala
800

Panama
3,800

Ecuador
1,000

Cuba
1,000

Colombia
7,000

Venezuela
20,000

Brazil
150,000

Peru
5,000

Bolivia
600

Paraguay
900

Chile
17,000

Uruguay
44,000

Argentina
228,000

Austria	12,000
Belgium	30,000
Bulgaria	5,000
Czechoslovakia	12,000
Greece	4,875
Hungary	90,000
Italy	35,000
Netherlands	25,000
Portugal	300
Romania	23,000
Switzerland	18,300
Syria	4,000
Former Yugoslavia	5,500

DIFFERENT BUT SIMILAR

Sephardic and Ashkenazic Jews each have their own customs and pronounce Hebrew differently, but they practice Judaism in similar ways.

In Israel there about as many Sephardim as there are Ashkenazim. Elsewhere, Ashkenazic Jews far outnumber Sephardic Jews.

ASHKENAZIM

Jews whose families originate in northern, central, and eastern Europe are known as Ashkenazic Jews. Many Ashkenazic communities spoke a language called Yiddish for centuries. It is based on old German, with words from other languages, such as Polish, but is written in the Hebrew script. Small numbers of Jews still speak Yiddish and some Jews are trying to keep it from dying out.

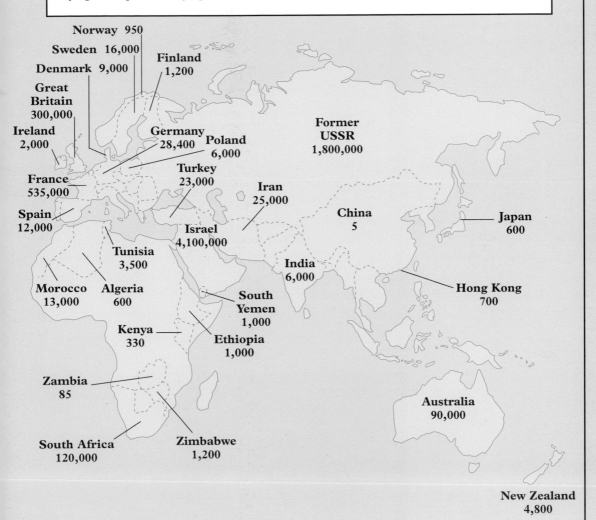

Norway 950
Sweden 16,000
Denmark 9,000
Finland 1,200
Great Britain 300,000
Ireland 2,000
Germany 28,400
Poland 6,000
Former USSR 1,800,000
France 535,000
Turkey 23,000
Iran 25,000
China 5
Japan 600
Spain 12,000
Israel 4,100,000
India 6,000
Hong Kong 700
Tunisia 3,500
Morocco 13,000
Algeria 600
South Yemen 1,000
Kenya 330
Ethiopia 1,000
Zambia 85
Australia 90,000
South Africa 120,000
Zimbabwe 1,200
New Zealand 4,800

SEPHARDIM

Jews from southern Europe, the Middle East, and further south are called Sephardic Jews. Many Sefardic communities in southern Europe spoke a language called Ladino for centuries. It is similar to old Spanish. Very few Jews speak Ladino today.

Jewish immigrants from Ethiopia are given temporary housing together for a while, where they learn Hebrew and get used to Israel's ways of life. Then they find their own homes.

A LONG JOURNEY

In 1984, as famine there grew worse, the Berak family escaped from Ethiopia. As they traveled, bandits attacked them and stole their donkey, food, and water. They became sick. When someone died, they were too afraid to stop to bury him. They carried on because it would be worse to turn back. Eventually they were put on a plane—the first they had ever seen—and taken to Israel. This was part of the Israeli rescue mission called "Operation Moses."

The Beraks were taken care of in Israel. They learned Hebrew and how to use modern appliances. They found stores, buses, running water, and electricity very strange at first. Moshe Berak says: "Israeli life is so different. I don't think many people really understand our culture and this makes it hard to mix. In Ethiopia we were nicknamed *Falasha*—which means strangers—and people swore at us a lot. But we have always called ourselves *Beta Yisrael*—the House of Israel—and that is why I am glad to be in Israel, with my people."

Young Jewish people at a camp run by the Women's International Zionist Organization.

3

JEWISH WRITINGS

"People of the book"

Jews are sometimes called "the people of the book," because Jewish writings are so important to them. Many Jewish homes have lots of books—on Judaism and other subjects. Jews use the terms *speaking* and *hearing* to express the way they understand God. They do not mean that God physically has a voice and ears, but that is how they describe how God and people communicate with each other. Jews feel that God is also expressed in the beauty of nature and in the love among people.

A young man in the Ukraine is immersed in the weekly Torah portion. He reads the text and commentaries from a humash. *The man in the background stands to say his morning prayers.*

What is the Torah?

Torah is "teaching" and the word is used in several ways. The Sefer Torah is a scroll or book containing the first five books of the Bible. *Torah* also means all

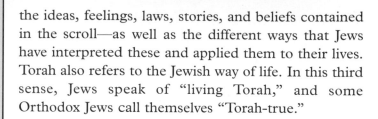

LOVE YOUR NEIGHBOR

One of the most important sayings in the Torah is: "Be holy for I, the Lord your God, am holy…Love your neighbor as yourself: I am the Lord."
(Leviticus 19: 2, 18)

the ideas, feelings, laws, stories, and beliefs contained in the scroll—as well as the different ways that Jews have interpreted these and applied them to their lives. Torah also refers to the Jewish way of life. In this third sense, Jews speak of "living Torah," and some Orthodox Jews call themselves "Torah-true."

Stories and sayings

The Torah has many stories about the children of Israel and the way they hear God through their experiences and relationships. Some of the stories are about everyday things or normal family life, but some of the events and experiences hold special significance for the children of Israel.

The Ten Sayings

The Torah contains 613 commandments through which God speaks to the children of Israel about how to worship and how to live. Not all the commandments apply to everyone all the time. Some apply only in Israel, and those to do with the First Temple do not apply at all today.

The most important commandments are the Ten Sayings. Most synagogues have these clearly written, in Hebrew, on a wall plaque. Usually just the first phrase of each saying is given, and often the first five and second five Sayings are shown as two lists, on two stones or sheets. This format reminds Jews of the tradition that Moses received the Ten Sayings written on two stones or tablets on Mount Sinai.

The American-born artist Philip Ratner has depicted the Ten Sayings in ten paintings. "You shall not commit adultery" (top) shows features of the wedding ceremony. The four angels hold the canopy. "Respect your father and mother so that the days of your life be fulfilled" is shown as a series of generations in a family.

Understanding the Torah

Traditionally, Jews have thought of the Torah as a letter from God, but some Orthodox and most Conservative and Progressive Jews today see the influence of people in the creation of the Torah. They think that the Torah was passed on by word of mouth for a long time before it was written down. But, however Jews understand the Torah, they all use exactly the same text.

Sephardim in Middle Eastern countries traditionally have a wooden or metal case for the Torah. This boy has become Bar Mitzvah and is reading during the morning service at the Western Wall.

Written and oral Torah

By the time of the exile in Babylon, at least part of the Torah had been written down and was being read to the people. They discussed what it meant, and wise people explained it to them. By the time of the rabbis, these discussions became very important and are called the oral Torah. This was remembered and eventually written down as the Talmud (study). Traditional Jews believe that the oral Torah was given to Moses at the same time as the written Torah, but that it took many hundreds of years to be discovered through discussion.

WAYS OF SEEING THE TORAH

There are several ways to see the Torah and how it came to the Jewish people:

A letter from God
God spoke the Torah directly to Moses, Moses wrote it down completely and exactly, and no word of the Torah has ever changed or can ever change.

A mental message from God
The *ideas* of the Torah were given to Moses and he wrote them down in human words.

A diary of the people
The Torah was created by people who believed in God and recorded their experiences.

A compilation
The Torah is put together as it goes along and contains different kinds of material, including records of later thoughts.

"If I am not for myself, who will be for me? But if I am only for myself, what am I? And, if not now, when?" (Hillel)

"You do not have to finish the work but you are not free to neglect it!" (Tarfon)

"Who is wise? The one who learns from everyone. Who is strong? The one who controls oneself. Who is rich? The one who is happy with what he has. Who is honorable? The one who honors others." (Ben Zoma)

A silver yad

Pirke Avot

The Talmud is a large collection of books. One of the best-known is the Pirke Avot (Chapters of the Ancestors or Sayings of the Fathers), which is made up of short sayings. In most of the Talmud, people who had particular ideas are not usually named, but in the Pirke Avot they are. Some of the sayings have been set to music and are loved by young Jewish people.

Reading the Torah

Reading the Torah is a regular part of Jewish community worship. There is a portion of the Torah for each week and, in a year, the whole Torah is read from beginning to end. There are also portions for festivals.

The Torah is always read in Hebrew from a scroll, exactly as it is written. Because the letters are close together, a pointer called a *yad* (hand) is sometimes used to help the reader to follow the text without smudging the writing. A Torah scroll is always written by hand by a trained scribe, who takes enormous care to make the lines straight and even. Sometimes the scribe has to make the letters near the end of a line large to ensure that the words fill the line.

TeNaKh

The Jewish Bible is made up of the **T**orah, the **N**evi'im (prophets, such as Jeremiah), and the **K**etuvim (Writings, including the Psalms). The initials of the three parts make TeNaKh, which is the name for the Jewish Bible. A part of the Nevi'im is read after every weekly Torah portion. Parts of the Ketuvim are read at certain festivals, and psalms are sung at any time.

The TeNaKh is almost the same as the Christian Old Testament, but Jews dislike that name for their Bible. To them, it is not old, but always fresh and alive.

The Torah is the life and soul of the party on Simchat Torah and on occasions such as the completion of writing a scroll.

LOVING THE TORAH

When the Romans occupied the land of Israel in the first century C.E., they forbade Jews to study the Torah, on pain of death. Rabbi Akiva told this parable:

A fox called to a fish from the riverbank, and said "It must be very cold and dark in there. There are stones on the bottom and the water gets rough in places. But up here, it's lovely. Why don't you get out and we can play together?" The fish knew she could not survive out of water and that the fox was trying to trick her. So she replied, "I like my river and it's my home. It's hard for me to live in a place I know, but it would be even harder to live in a place I don't know!" And she swam away.

Rabbi Akiva said that the fox was like the Romans, the fish like the Jews, and the river like the Torah. It may have been hard for Jews to live with the Torah when the Romans were there, but it would have been even harder without the Torah.

This midrash is one of the oldest and is well known by Jewish children. It explores how Abraham turned away from idol worship:

Abraham's father was an idol merchant and left him in charge of the store one day. Abraham looked at all the statues, of different sizes and materials, then took a large hammer and smashed them one by one—all but the very biggest. His father was furious with him but Abraham pointed to the big idol and said, "That one did it!"

"Don't be stupid!" replied his father. "It couldn't possibly... Idols have no power!"

"Then why do you worship them?"

Humash

Few individual Jews have a Torah scroll, but many have a *humash*. This is a book of the weekly portions of the Torah, with a translation and explanation of each one, and the reading from the Nevi'im that goes with it. Jews always study the Torah with a commentary—notes written by learned people in the past and present. In this way, they are part of the ongoing tradition of the Torah—and not just individuals trying to understand what it means on their own. Many Jews in synogogue follow the Torah reading from a *humash*.

All Jews are encouraged to take time each day to study and pray. Many synagogues create an informal atmosphere where people can feel at ease. The seating in this Tunisian synagogue makes it easy to get comfortable. This elderly Jew relaxes with a book.

Midrash

A midrash (explanation) is a story to explain and explore something in the Bible. Midrashim (plural) developed at about the same time as the Talmud and were recorded in books. Jews continuously make midrashim.

4

THE JEWISH HOME

In many homes, Jews put money into a charity box before Shabbat and festivals. This girl's family collects for tree planting in Israel.

Home is important to Jews. Events in a person's life and all festivals are celebrated or commemorated at home, and the synagogue takes second place. It is mostly through the home that children learn about their religion, history, and culture. They learn by doing things such as touching the mezuzah at the doorways to their homes and kissing their fingers, putting coins into the charity box, helping to prepare for Shabbat, and, more formally, discussing religious texts, especially at mealtimes.

LEARNING AND LIVING

Ester Gluck is 12 years old. Like many Jewish children, she cannot remember when she learned she was Jewish. It seems as if she always knew.

Ester has kept the mezuzah-kissing custom since she was a toddler. One day, on reaching home, she cried, "Kiss 'zuzah!" and insisted on being lifted up—even though her mother had armfuls of groceries and was rummaging for her keys!

When it was her turn at nursery school to bring home the rabbits for the winter vacation, Ester learned the Talmudic teaching that Jews should feed their animals before themselves. So every morning she marched out into the snow to give the rabbits cabbage—and then she had her own breakfast.

Ester knew the blessing for bread when she was only two. "What really matters," her mother says, "is whether she still says it when she's twenty-two and whether she teaches it to her children when they're two!"

THE SHEMA

The reason the Shema is put on doorposts is given in the Shema itself:

Hear, O Israel, the Lord is our God. The Lord is one. Love the Lord your God with all your heart, and with all your soul, and with all your might. These words that I command you today shall be upon your heart. Teach them to your children, and talk about them when you sit in your house, and when you walk in the street, when you lie down and when you rise up. Hold fast to them as a sign upon your hand, and let them be as reminders before your eyes. Write them on the doorposts of your house and on your gates. (Deuteronomy 6: 4–9)

The mezuzah

On the doorway to Jewish homes are mezuzahs, tiny boxes, each containing a piece of scroll. On the scroll are written the words of the Shema, which is one of the most important passages in the Torah and a prayer recited evening and morning. The custom of touching the mezuzah and kissing the fingers, on the way in and out of the door, is a sign of love for what the writing means and the value of the home.

The Old City of Jerusalem is walled, with eight gates, and in many ways it is like a huge house. A tourist pauses at the Jaffa Gate to touch the mezuzah and kiss her fingers.

The table

Modern life affects Jews as much as others and they, too, may have breakfast standing up in the kitchen or TV dinners. But most Jewish families try to eat together at least once a day and always on Shabbat. Observant Jews say a blessing over food to show that they are grateful to God and others for what they are about to eat. For instance, the blessing for bread is: "Blessed are you, Lord our God, ruler of the universe, who brings forth bread from the earth."

Kashrut—rules about food

Rules about what Jews may eat, called kashrut, mainly come from the Torah. Food that Jews are allowed to eat is called kosher (meaning "proper" or "fit"). Orthodox Jews observe the laws about food strictly—at home and when out. For Progressive Jews, the laws are less important and some may observe them only partly; for example, only by not eating pork or shellfish. Today many Jews keep kosher homes, but not always when out with non-Jewish friends.

Meat, milk, and other foods

Birds and mammals must be killed with a single, swift cut by a trained *shochet* (slaughterer), who cares about the animals' feelings and about Jewish laws. Meat that has not been prepared like this is called *tref* (torn or strangled). *Tref* is also used for all nonkosher food.

To make meat kosher, the blood must be removed by soaking, salting, and rinsing. This is because the blood is thought to contain the animal's life essence. Koshering the meat can be done by the butcher or by someone at home.

Meat and milk must not be eaten together. This comes from a verse in the Torah: "Do not stew a kid in its mother's milk." It reminds Jews of the feelings between the mother and her baby. Meat symbolizes death and milk symbolizes life, so they are not mixed. Orthodox Jews have separate sets of crockery and cutlery for milk and meat foods. They may even have separate refrigerators for milk and meat foods and separate dishwashers for the two sets of crockery and cutlery.

Most foods are neither milk nor meat and are called pareve. They include eggs from kosher birds, fish, and food from plants. Jews may eat pareve food with meat or with milk or by itself.

Kashrut is complicated in the modern world because there are so many processed foods with additives that may be *tref*. Some Jewish food producers ask a rabbi to

KASHRUT

Kashrut is more a formula than a list of foods. For example, Jews may eat:

 fish that have fins and scales. Cod is kosher, but shrimp are not.

 the meat of birds that eat grain, but not birds of prey. Chickens are kosher, but owls are not.

 the meat of mammals that have split hooves and chew their cuds. Sheep are kosher, but pigs are not.

 any edible plants, the milk of kosher animals, and the eggs of kosher birds.

supervise production to certify that the food is kosher, so that Jews will know they may eat it. Rabbis also analyze other products and issue lists of brand names that are kosher. Orthodox Jews refer to these lists when shopping. In Israel, keeping kosher is easy, because most food stores stock only kosher products.

In most homes, Jews stand to sing "kiddush" (a ceremonial prayer over bread or wine) on Shabbat. The white tablecloth symbolizes the Shabbat as a bride. This family has the custom of singing kiddush with one cup of wine, which the father holds. He then pours a little wine into each cup for the family and guests.

Men and women

Men and women have different roles in Jewish ritual. For example, the woman usually lights candles for Shabbat, but the man says the blessing over the bread. Men's and women's roles are valued. At home, either or both may cook, polish the candlesticks for Shabbat, or bathe the baby, and both may contribute to the family income.

Parents and children

One of the Ten Sayings is "Honor your father and mother," but there is no saying "Honor your children." One explanation is that parents instinctively respect and love their children, but it does not come naturally to children to respect and love their parents—and so they have to be told to do so!

It is the last night of Hanukkah. All eight candles and the shammes (helper or servant) candle in the menorah (candleholder) have been lit, and it is time for a familiar festival story. The shammes candle is used to light all the others.

FROM GENERATION TO GENERATION

This midrash is about parents and children and the need to care for future generations:

As the rain fell heavily and the waters rose, a family of birds was afraid of drowning in the flood. So the father bird flew with his young on his back—one at a time—from their nest toward a dry place. Halfway across, he asked the first baby, "When I am old, will you care for me as I care for you?" The baby answered, "Yes, of course, father!" This was not the answer he hoped for—and he dropped the little bird into the water below. He asked the second one the same question, got the same answer—and did the same thing. Halfway across, he asked the third, "When I am old, will you care for me as I care for you?" This one replied, "I don't know, father...but I hope I shall care for *my* children as you care for me!" The father carried his baby lovingly to a new nest.

THE JEWISH COMMUNITY

Home is so important in the Jewish tradition that the synagogue, the main community institution, is called *bet*, meaning "house." Each has three Hebrew names and each name conveys one of its uses. Many North American Jews call the synagogue the temple.

A house of gathering

In Israel, *bet knesset* (house of gathering) is the most common name. Synagogues all around the world are used for many activities, such as parties, fund-raising events, meetings of volunteer workers, day centers for the elderly or disabled, and toddler groups. Most synagogues have a kitchen and toilets, and many have offices where the synagogue's work is organized.

Some young Jewish people go to the synagogue during the week to attend classes given by their rabbi.

A house of learning

Yiddish-speaking Jews call the synagogue *shul* (school). The Hebrew name is *bet midrash*, which means "house of study."

Synagogues provide many opportunities for Jews to learn. The most important is the weekly reading of the Torah. This may be followed by a sermon given by the rabbi or another member of the congregation. A sermon is called a *derasha*, which is another form of the word for "study."

Shabbat, which lasts from Friday evening to Saturday evening, is the most important time of the week, and more Jews go to synagogue then than on weekdays. Shabbat is a rest day, when Jews study by reading and talking. For observant Jews, resting includes not writing, using computers, painting, cutting, bathing...So religion classes for children and young people are usually held on Sundays (and sometimes after school).

Most synagogues offer classes for adults on topics from reading Hebrew to baking bread. Progressive synagogues, in particular, create opportunities for families to learn together informally through games, quizzes, and drama activities. These often take the form of a Family Day.

"A Lifeline to the Aged" is a workshop program in Israel through which retired people can learn and develop skills, talk to others of their age group, and earn money by selling what they make. This man learned pottery and says, "A whole world opened up to me."

A LOT OF FUN

Desi Tammam's family is Sephardic, from Libya, and lives in Britain. Desi is in her late teens. She says: "A youth group is held in the 'House' where there are activities for age groups four to twenty-five—all sorts of role plays and discussions, about the Holocaust or Soviet Jews or how we feel when we get called names in the street. There are vacation camps, too. The youngest children sleep in buildings, but the teenagers are in tents. It's a lot of fun!"

In Orthodox synagogues, men and women study separately; in Progressive synagogues, they study together. In recent years, more women have studied together than before. When Moses was on Mount Sinai receiving the Torah, the men became impatient and wanted to make a golden calf to worship as an idol —but the women refused to contribute their jewelry! The new moon became a women's festival as their reward for not worshiping idols. The celebration almost entirely died away, but some women are reviving it. They meet for study, as well as prayer, song, and the sharing of food.

A house of prayer

Another Hebrew name for the synagogue is *bet t'filah* (house of prayer). The Hebrew word for prayer, *filah*, comes from a word meaning "to judge oneself." Jews may pray alone, but they are encouraged to pray with other Jews. They do not need to be in a synagogue. Most prayers say "we," "us," and "our," rather than "I," "me," and "my"—and "you" when addressing God. A minyan is a group of ten or more adult males, the number traditionally required for a service to be public. If there is no

The Torah is carried around the synagogue as the congregation sings psalms. Many people come close and touch it with the fringes of their prayer shawls. An Ashkenazic scroll has a removable velvet cover. The bells jingle softly so that everyone can hear as well as see the Torah.

minyan, Orthodox Jews leave out some prayers from their service. This rule encourages Orthodox Jews to want to join in the service, because they are needed. Progressive communities do not count a minyan.

The rabbi and the hazan

Some synagogues do not have a rabbi; some synagogues have more than one rabbi; and some rabbis work in more than one synagogue. Nowadays, rabbis are paid for the work they do, and most do not have other jobs. Rabbis are qualified to teach and to judge, but they also give people advice with problems and comfort them when they are troubled. In Orthodox communities, only men can become rabbis. Some Progressive and Conservative rabbis are women.

Most Orthodox and Conservative communities have a *hazan*, a trained singer who leads the sung parts of the prayers and often chants the Torah portion. Many Progressive communities have choirs of men and women. Orthodox choirs are less common and are always male.

"Know before whom you stand" is the inscription over the Ark in this British Orthodox synagogue. Above it are the Ten Sayings. Usually the bimah *(platform) is in the middle of the congregation and faces the Ark, although here it is at the front. In most synagogues, as here, there are seats at the side so that people face in and can see one another. This gives a feeling of oneness.*

33

The siddur (prayer book) was first compiled in the eighth century and is still being developed. Its structure is basically the same throughout the Jewish world, but there are variations. For example, some Sephardic prayer books include Ladino prayers, and Progressive prayer books do not refer to temple sacrifices.

"God said 'Let there be light' and there was light...God called the light day and he called the darkness night..." These verses from the book of Genesis have been written here by artist and scribe Gordon Charatan. He rounded the Hebrew letters at the ends of each line to make the circle.

Services

The Jewish day begins at sunset and has three services: evening, morning, and afternoon. These come from the times when priests offered sacrifices in the temple. On Shabbat and festivals, there is an additional service after the morning service.

In Orthodox synagogues, the weekly Torah portion is read on Monday, Thursday, and Saturday mornings; in Progressive synagogues, only on Saturday mornings.

The prayer book, called the siddur (order), contains Psalms and prayers from the Bible, as well as later compositions. It is mostly in Hebrew, sometimes with a translation into the everyday language. In Progressive and some Conservative services, some of the prayers are said in translation.

In Orthodox synagogues, men and women sit separately, and children may sit with either. Women are usually upstairs or behind a screen. In Progressive synagogues, men, women, and children sit together. Some Conservative synagogues have separate seating, and others mixed.

6

IMPORTANT CEREMONIES

Welcoming a baby

When a Jewish boy is eight days old, he is circumcised. A *mohel*, a specially trained person who is often a Jewish doctor or surgeon, removes the foreskin of the boy's penis. Because the baby's nervous system is not fully developed, the pain is far less than it would be for an older boy. This simple ritual often takes place in the synagogue or home and is followed by a party. The Torah commands Jewish parents to have their sons circumcised, to show that they have entered the covenant, or promise, of Abraham. The celebration of this commandment is called Brit Milah (the covenant of cutting). Family and friends say, "Just as he has entered into the covenant, so may he also enter into the blessings of Torah, of marriage, and of good deeds."

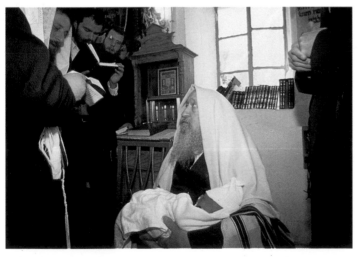

A Brit Milah in a synagogue. There is more room there than in a home, and the occasion becomes a community event.

Parents also take their baby to synagogue to announce its name. The community welcomes its new member.

NAMES

Jewish parents will name their new baby after a member of their family or someone in Jewish history, or they will choose a name that points to qualities that they hope the child will grow up to have. In Ashkenazic custom, children are named after dead relatives; but in Sephardic custom, they can be named after living relatives.

Every Jew has a Hebrew name, which is used in many Jewish rituals and appears on Jewish documents. His or her Hebrew name is used when he or she is called to the Torah, married, or buried. Outside Israel, Jews also have "everyday" names, which may be quite different from their Hebrew names.

This is part of a prayer said by Progressive Jewish girls. There is also a version for a Bar Mitzvah.

"…I now prepare to take upon myself the duties which are binding on all the family of Israel…I think of those who have gone before me, who through all the troubles of the world preserved this heritage of holiness and goodness, so that I should enter into it now. May I be a true Bat Mitzvah…May I be a witness to the living God and his goodness, and the tradition that lives within me."

A Bat Mitzvah-to-be, encouraged by her rabbi, reads the Torah text for the last time before chanting it to the congregation the following morning.

Growing up

In the Jewish tradition, girls are considered adult at the age of twelve and boys at thirteen. These young adults are responsible for obeying the commandments. Since the Middle Ages, the custom has developed of marking the stage when a boy becomes a man by inviting him to lead the congregation in prayer or to read the weekly Torah portion. He is called a Bar Mitzvah (son of the divine law). It has become a big event, especially in North America.

A blessing is pronounced as a boy is bar mitzvahed.

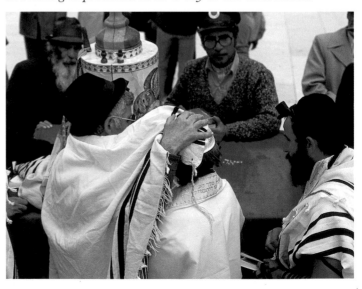

In 1923 in a Progressive synagogue in New York City, a girl was called to the Torah for the first time as a Bat Mitzvah (daughter of the divine law). Since then, many Progressive Jewish girls have celebrated becoming Bat Mitzvahs in the same way as boys.

Orthodox Jewish girls have also begun to celebrate coming of age, but in a different way from Progressive girls and boys and Orthodox boys. Often, the name given is Bat Hayil (daughter of valor) and a group of girls have a joint celebration at which they read psalms and poetry. It is not part of a normal service, but a separate occasion.

The final run-through for the big day. Tomorrow Libby will be bat mitzvahed and take her place in the congregation as a Jewish woman.

A SPECIAL DAY AT A SPECIAL TIME

Solomon Sananes comes from a large, close-knit Egyptian Sephardic family. "I was bar mitzvahed in 1967. It was a year of tough studying, but we managed to have fun, too! It was nerve-racking going up to the *bimah* (platform), even though I had had a run-through the day before. Family came from far and wide and we had an open house right after the service for the rabbi, relatives, and friends. The main function was on the Sunday evening. I was perhaps too young and overwhelmed to take it in—but it was a very happy occasion. Some people gave my parents a bit of flak, saying that all the money they spent should have gone to Israel, because of the Six-Day War three months earlier. But my parents felt that what they gave to charity was their business, that joyous events are important in Jewish life, and that they could support Israel *and* celebrate their son's Bar Mitzvah."

Marriage

The basic Jewish wedding ceremony is simple. It is a combination of two ceremonies: the betrothal and the marriage. Customs throughout the world make the ceremony beautiful, interesting, and more complex. But it is first of all a binding agreement between the man and the woman, made in the presence of witnesses. The man gives the woman a *ketubah* (marriage contract), which states that he will look after her. To show that she is willing to marry him, the woman points the index finger of her right hand and he puts a ring on it, saying, "By this ring, you are married to me in holiness according to the law of Moses and of Israel."

The wedding takes place under a *huppah* (canopy), which symbolizes the home. The ceremony itself is called *huppah v'kiddushin* (canopy and holiness). Ideally, the *huppah* is outside, but can also be in a home or synagogue. The bride is usually veiled at first,

The ketubah *is a binding legal agreement and often a work of art, too. The round shape symbolizes the eternity of love, and the motif here is the walls of Jerusalem. The* ketubah *becomes the bride's property, and she will probably frame it and hang it up at home.*

but her veil is lifted as she is revealed to her husband. The couple share wine. A hazan, choir, or friends sing seven blessings, which include "Give these companions in love great happiness, the happiness of your creatures in Eden long ago. Blessed are you, Lord, who rejoices the bridegroom and the bride."

At the end of the ceremony, the husband smashes a glass with his foot. This symbolizes the destruction of the Temple, which shattered the Jewish people. It also reminds Jews that life is fragile and that even happy moments can be tinged with sadness. When they hear the broken glass, all the guests shout "Mazel tov!" (Good luck!)

David Gryn painted this vibrant yet intimate picture of a bride and groom as a gift for his sister when she got married.

Death and mourning

When someone dies, those who knew and loved him or her are encouraged to express their feelings. Men and women are allowed to cry freely. Jews think it is silly and unhealthy for someone not to cry when feeling sad. Many of the customs around Jewish funerals are meant to help people grieve and also to help them gradually back to a life without the one who died.

Jewish funerals take place as soon as possible after death, usually on the same or the following day. It is considered disrespectful to the dead to leave the body unburied any longer than necessary. Most Jews are buried, but some Progressive Jews are cremated.

The dead person is washed and carefully wrapped in a white garment. A man who regularly wore a tallith (prayer shawl) will be dressed in it for burial. Sometimes the body is placed in a coffin for burial and sometimes

THE KADDISH

This prayer does not mention death at all, but praises God as the giver of life: "Let us magnify and let us sanctify the great name of God in the world which he created according to his will. May his kingdom come in your lifetime, and in your days, and in the lifetime of the family of Israel—quickly and speedily may it come... He is far beyond any blessing or song, any honor, or any consolation that can be spoken of in this world."

it is placed directly in the ground. Close mourners often throw the first shovelfuls of soil into the grave. A cemetery is called *bet hayim* (house of life) or *bet olam* (house of eternity). As people leave, they may wash their hands, symbolizing that they are leaving death behind and are returning to the world of life.

For a week, friends and family meet to comfort one another and say prayers in the home of the person who has died. This is called sitting shiva. Close family members do not have to go to work or school for a week and are not be expected to do anything. The idea is that people need to grieve without worrying about anything else, and grieving makes people tired. Friends and relatives do whatever the mourners need.

When visiting a Jewish grave to remember and pay respects to the dead, it is a custom to leave a small stone as a mark of the visit and a sign of the harsh reality of death.

For almost a year, close mourners recite Kaddish (holy prayer) every day. Within a year of the death, the gravestone is erected. Sephardic gravestones lie flat over the grave, to show that in death everyone is equal. Ashkenazic gravestones are flat or upright. On every anniversary of the death, close mourners recite Kaddish and light a candle that burns all night and day.

7

THE JEWISH YEAR

Apples dipped in honey are eaten at Rosh Hashanah.

Through the year, festivals help Jews experience many customs and express emotions. The main festivals are shown on the chart on the next page.

The Jewish calendar

The Jewish calendar is made up of lunar months, which last from new moon to new moon. In ancient times, a month began when a new moon was sighted in Jerusalem. However, for centuries, Jewish scholars have calculated when new moons would come. Lunar months are 29 or 30 days long, so there are about twelve and a third in a year. To use the extra days and keep festivals in their season, some years have a "leap month."

Before the new moon could be calculated, Jews outside Israel did not know exactly when it would come, so they celebrated it over two days. They also observed the festivals given in the Torah for two days—except Yom Kippur. Orthodox Jews outside Israel keep the tradition of double-day celebrations, but Progressive Jews and Israeli Jews keep just one day.

A family in their sukkah for the festival of Sukkot. The father holds the "four species," including the sweet-smelling yellow etrog.

THE MOST WIDELY CELEBRATED

English and Hebrew Names	Time (Approximate)	What the festival commemorates, or how it began
Passover Pesach	7–8 days in March/April	The Israelites' escape from slavery in Egypt.
Holocaust Remembrance Day Yom Ha'Shoah	1 day in April	The destruction of six million Jews and thousands of communities by the Nazis during the Holocaust. Day of memorial decreed by the Israeli parliament.
Israel Independence Day Yom Ha'Atzmaut	1 day in April/May	The creation of the State of Israel.
Festival of Weeks Shavuot	1–2 days in June	The giving of the Torah to Moses on Mount Sinai.
Ninth of Av Tisha B'Av	1 day in August	The destruction of the First Temple and the second temple—and other Jewish tragedies.
New Year Rosh Hashanah	1–2 days in September	Newness. A day of blowing the shofar (ram's horn).
Day of Atonement Yom Kippur	1 day in September/October	Repentance. Before the destruction of the Second Temple, the high priest made atonement for people on this day.
Festival of Booths/ Tabernacles—Sukkot	7–8 days in September/October	The children of Israel building booths in the wilderness after escaping from Egypt.
8th day of Sukkot/ Rejoicing in Torah Shemini Atzeret/Simchat Torah	1–2 days in September/October	The 8th day is given in the Torah, but the Simchat Torah celebration developed in the Middle Ages as a finale to Sukkot.
Festival of Rededication Hanukkah	8 days in December	Restoration of Temple worship by the Maccabees after it had been spoiled by enemy idol-worshipers.
New Year of Trees Tu B'Shvat	1 day in January	Care for the environment. Dating from the Talmudic period, it marks the time when fruit of trees begins to form.
Festival of Lots Purim	1 day in February/March	Esther, Jewish queen of Persia, risking her life to save her people from the king's prime minister, Haman.

☐ Given in the Torah ☐ Modern
☐ Decreed by Jewish leaders in ancient times

FESTIVALS AND FASTS IN THE JEWISH YEAR

Day of rest?	How Jews celebrate
First and last days	No foods containing leaven are eaten and Jews eat matzoh instead of ordinary bread. A seder (Passover supper) is held on the 1st or 2nd evening, with songs and stories from a book called the Haggadah (Telling). Symbolic foods evoke the experience of captivity and freedom.
No	Especially important in Israel and among North American and European Jews. Jews gather to remember, mourn, and strengthen themselves to prevent such tragedies in the future. Readings from Holocaust literature, specially composed prayers, songs from the Holocaust period.
No, but a public holiday in Israel	Public parades and parties in Israel and parties in Jewish communities elsewhere, with Israeli food and songs, including the Israeli national anthem, "HaTikvah" (Hope).
Yes	Studying—all night by some people. Eating dairy foods, decorating homes and synagogues with flowers. Reading Torah, including the Ten Sayings.
No	Reading the Book of Lamentations. Fasting completely for a day—including not wearing leather.
Yes	Blowing the shofar for spiritual awakening. Synagogue cloths in white and some people in white clothes. Eating apples and honey, honey cakes and "new" fruits. Sending New Year cards. Asking forgiveness for past year, before Yom Kippur.
Yes	Total fast for 25 hours. Lighting candles at home, which burn for 25 hours. Congregation in synagogue make confessions to God. Synagogue cloths in white and white clothes worn by some people. Blowing shofar at end of fast.
First day(s)	Families build sukkot (temporary, fragile booths) and take their meals in them for a week. Shaking the lulav (date palm), myrtle, and willow of the brook. Blessing the *etrog*.
Yes	Taking meals in sukkot, but not shaking the lulav. Parading Torah scrolls in synagogues and in the streets. Reading the end and the beginning of the Torah, because the Torah is continuous.
No	Lighting candles each night for eight nights—one on first night, two on second night…Eating foods cooked in oil, such as latkes (potato pancakes) and doughnuts. Playing a game with a dreidl (special spinning top).
No, but special events in Israeli schools	Planting or sponsoring the planting of saplings in Israel. Outside Israel, tasting 15 fruits.
No, but school holiday in Israel	Reading the Book of Esther and trying to make enough noise to drown out the name of Haman. Wearing costumes. Eating hamantashen (sweet, triangular pastries filled with fruit).

This Yemenite family at Pesach has set out the matzoh and the symbolic foods for the seder. The bone and roasted egg recall sacrifices in the Temple. A paste of nuts, dates, apples, and wine, called charoset, *is a reminder of the mortar the slaves used while building in Egypt. Romaine lettuce or horseradish represent bitterness. Vinegar or salt water is for sadness and suffering. A green vegetable symbolizes springtime and hope.*

Shabbat

The most important festival of all is Shabbat, a day for peace and rest that comes every week. Other festivals are observed in many of the same ways as Shabbat is observed.

During the week, in preparation for Shabbat, Jews buy all the food they will need and clean the house thoroughly. On Friday, families come home in time to get ready and put the final touches on the food and table.

Traditionally, the table is set with a white cloth, two or more candles, wine or grape juice, and one or more special glasses or cups for kiddush (a prayer over wine, on the themes of creation and freedom). There will also be two loaves of bread called challah, which are made of a special dough and often braided; a cover for the challah; salt; and usually flowers, as well.

The theme of Shabbat is the God-Torah-Israel relationship, and the braided loaves symbolize this. Shabbat has three phases, each with a meal and each emphasizing one of the strands. On Friday evening, the theme is Israel, with friends and family enjoying one another's company and relaxing at the end of the week. The mood is lighthearted and the songs sung during the meal are happy ones. On Saturday morning there is the Torah reading at synagogue, which Jews often discuss over lunch. The afternoon is the God-time, when the feeling is more private. Jews go for walks, read, take naps, talk quietly, or just think personal thoughts.

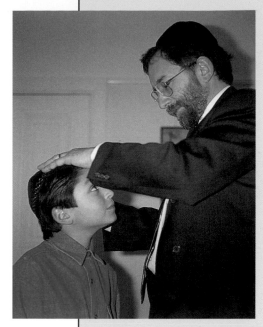

"May God make you like Ephraim and Manasseh" —two sons of Jacob. As a father blesses his son on a Friday evening, he wishes him all that is good.

When Shabbat is over on Saturday evening, the havdalah service marks the separation of rest and work and takes Jews back into the working week. Because fire symbolizes work, havdalah begins with the lighting of a braided candle. The candle again brings together the three themes of Shabbat. A box of sweet spices is passed around and sniffed, so that the fragrance and sweetness of Shabbat may linger, and there is wine for gladness. There is a legend that the prophet Elijah will return to herald the days of the Messiah when the world will be at peace. The final song yearns for him to come soon and to bring forever the day that has just been glimpsed on Shabbat. Then everyone wishes each other *"Shavua Tov!"*—"Have a good week!"

Havdalah can be made at any time after Shabbat until Tuesday evening. These young people, meeting for Jewish classes on a Sunday morning, start with havdalah and wish one another a good week.

Glossary

aliyah	"Going up": emigrating to Israel; being called up to read the Torah.	**Jerusalem**	The capital city of Israel. It is also called "Zion," after the hill on which it was built.
Ashkenazi	A Jew whose origins are from northern or eastern Europe.	**kashrut**	Jewish food laws. Food that Jews may eat is called kosher.
Bar Mitzvah	"Son of the divine law": a boy who is thirteen years old and is entering the Jewish community.	*ketubah*	A marriage document that the bridegroom gives to the bride.
Bat Mitzvah	"Daughter of the divine law": a girl who is twelve years old or, in a Progressive community, thirteen, and is entering the Jewish community.	**kosher**	"Fit, proper"; fit for use.
		Liberal	See Progressive and Reform.
Brit Milah	Ritual circumcision marking a boy's entry into the covenant with God.	**Messiah**	"The anointed one" who Jews believe will one day bring a perfect age for everyone that will last forever.
Conservative	A form of Judaism, especially in North America, which has features of both Reform and of Orthodox Judaism.	**mezuzah**	A small box on doorposts containing quotes from scripture.
Hasidic	Literally, "pious." The Hasidic movement began in Poland in the eighteenth century and emphasized purity of heart and joyous devotion to the Torah.	**midrash**	"Explanation": a story that explains and explores ideas hidden in other stories, especially in the TeNaKh.
		Orthodox	Keeping the religion according to the halaka (law).
havdalah	"Separation"; a ceremony to mark the end of Shabbat.	**Progressive**	Reform or Liberal; interpreting Judaism in light of modern life.
hazan	A trained singer who leads services, especially in Orthodox and Conservative synagogues.	**rabbi**	A Jewish religious teacher who may preach and act as a judge. Many rabbis also do community work.
Hebrew	The ancient and modern language that unifies the Jewish people; the language of the Torah and prayer books; the everyday language of Israel.	**Reform**	A form of Judaism that emphasizes the teachings of the TeNaKh more than the Talmud and changes some of the features of Orthodox practice while keeping the essence of Judaism. See Progressive.
humash	A book containing the text of the Torah, with commentaries.		
Israel	The homeland of the Jewish people since ancient times; a name for the Jewish people.	**secular**	A term for Jewish people who are born Jews and identify with the Jewish people but do not practice the religion.

Sephardi	A Jew whose origins are from Spain or other Mediterranean or Middle Eastern countries. Sephardic Jews spoke Ladino for centuries. This language was similar to medieval Spanish.
Shabbat	The Jewish Sabbath day, which lasts from sunset on Friday until sunset on Saturday.
Shoah	"Whirlwind": the Holocaust.
shul	See synagogue.
synagogue	The Jewish place of study, prayer, and meeting. Ashkenazic Jews call it *shul*.
Talmud	"Study": a collection of writings, completed in 500 C.E., based on rabbis' discussions about right and wrong. It has two parts, the Mishnah and the Gemara.
Temple	The central place of Jewish worship in Jerusalem from 1000 B.C.E. to 70 C.E., where priests offered sacrifices.
TeNaKh	The Jewish Bible, consisting of the Torah, the Nevi'im (prophets), and the Ketuvim (writings).
Torah	The first five books of the Jewish Bible; Jewish teaching (ideas and values); the Jewish way of life.
Yiddish	Language spoken by Ashkenazic Jews for centuries, based on medieval German and written in the Hebrew alphabet.
Zionist	One who believes in the importance of the modern State of Israel, striving to improve the safety and welfare of Israel and to strengthen the society there.

Book List

Nonfiction

Burstein, Chaya. *The Jewish Kids Catalog.* Philadelphia: The Jewish Publication Society of America, 1983. (Facts, stories, and lots of activities.)

Frank, Anne. *Anne Frank: The Diary of a Young Girl.* New York: Doubleday, 1967.

Gates, Faye C. *Judaism.* New York: Facts on File, 1991.

Greenberg, Blu. *How to Run a Traditional Jewish Household.* New York: Fireside Paperbacks, 1985.

Huttenbach, Henry. *Jewish-Americans.* New York: Chelsea House, 1989.

James, Ian. *Israel.* Inside. New York: Franklin Watts, 1990.

Rutter, Jill. *Jewish Migrations.* Migrations. New York: Thomson Learning, 1994

Fiction

Aleichem, Sholom. *Holiday Tales of Sholom Aleichem,* selected and translated by Aliza Shevrin. New York: Aladdin, 1985. (Stories on festival themes, set in the Ukrainian Yiddish-speaking Jewish community of old Russia at the end of the nineteenth century.)

Banks, Lynne Reid. *One More River.* New York: Morrow Junior Books, 1992. (A Canadian girl goes to live in Israel just before the Six-Day War and forms a relationship with an Arab boy in a nearby village.)

Blume, Judy. *Are You There God? It's Me, Margaret.* New York: Dell Yearling, 1970. (A teenage girl with one Jewish and one Christian parent talks to God about growing up and her religious and cultural identity.)

Bush, Lawrence. *Emma Ansky-Levine and her Mitzvah-Machine.* New York: Union of American Hebrew Congregations Press, 1991. (A fantasy story about a machine that takes her on journeys into the world of Jewish life.)

Singer, Isaac Bashevis. *When Shlemiel Went to Warsaw and Other Stories.* New York: Farrar, Straus & Giroux, 1986. (Stories set in Eastern Europe.)

Note on Dates

Each religion has its own system for counting the years of human history. The starting point may be related to the birth or death of a special person or an important event. In everyday life, today, when different communities have dealings with one another, they need to use the same counting system for setting dates in the future and writing accounts of the past. The Western system is now used throughout the world. It is based on Christian beliefs about Jesus: A.D. (*Anno Domini* = in the year of our Lord) and B.C. (Before Christ). Members of the various world faiths use the common Western system, but, instead of A.D. and B.C., they say and write C.E. (in the Common Era) and B.C.E. (before the Common Era).

Index